What Is Wind?

Alan Trussell-Cullen

Dominie Press, Inc.

Publisher: Christine Yuen
Series Editors: Adria F. Klein & Alan Trussell-Cullen
Editors: Bob Rowland & Paige Sanderson
Illustrator: David Preston Smith
Designers: Gary Hamada & Lois Stanfield

Photo Credits: PhotoDisc (Page 14); SuperStock (pages 12, 16, and 18).

Published by:

ᴨ Dominie Press, Inc.

1949 Kellogg Avenue
Carlsbad, California 92008 USA

www.dominie.com

ISBN 0-7685-0575-5

Printed in Singapore

17 V0ZF 14 13

Table of Contents

What Is Wind?   4

Which Way Is the Wind Blowing?   6

How Strong Is the Wind?   8

Our Wind Log   10

Strong Winds   12

How Wind Helps Plants   14

How Wind Helps Us   16

Picture Glossary   20

Index   20

Wind is moving air.
We can't see air,
so we can't see wind.
But we can feel it
on our skin, and we can see
what it does.

We wanted to see which way
the wind was blowing.
We made a wind vane.

The wind can blow
to the north, or the south,
or the east, or the west.

We adapted the Beaufort Scale
to measure how strong the wind is

What the wind is doing ?	How strong is the Wind ?	How fast is the wind ?	
		miles per hour	kilometers per hour
	Wind force 0 No wind at all.	0-1	0-1
	Wind force: 2 A light breeze	4-7	6-11
	Wind force: 4 A moderate breeze	13-18	20-28
	Wind force: 6 A strong breeze	25-31	39-49
	Wind force: 8 A gale	39-48	62-74
	Windforce: 10 A terrible gale	55-63	89-102
	Wind force: 12 A hurricane	74+	117+

We can find out how strong the wind is by looking at what it does to things.

Our Wind log

Monday
Wind Direction East
Wind force 2

Tuesday
Wind Direction East
Wind force 0

Wednesday
Wind Direction South
Wind force 2

Thursday
Wind Direction East
Wind force 6

Friday
Wind Direction North.
Wind force 4

Saturday
Wind Direction West
Wind force 2

Sunday
Wind Direction West
Wind force 10

We kept a log of the wind for a week.

Winds can be good and bad for us.

Strong winds can be very bad.

But the wind can be good, too.
Plants often use the wind
to spread their seeds.

We use the wind, too.

It dries our clothes.

It turns windmills.

It pushes sailboats along.

The wind will even help me fly my kite.

Picture Glossary

kite:

wind vane:

sailboat:

windmill:

Index

Beaufort Scale, 8
breeze, 8

gale, 8

hurricane, 8

kite, 19

sailboat(s), 17
seeds, 15
strong winds, 13

wind log, 10
wind vane, 7
windmill(s), 17